The Hip Guru's Guide®

21 Days to Joy

Forgiving & Loving Your Body, Mind & Soul

By Swami Sadashiva Tirtha
Author of the Amazon #1 bestseller
in its category, *The Ayurveda Encyclopedia*

ISBN-978-0-9797445-4-9
ISBN-10: 0-9797445-4-7

Revised 2nd Edition 2017
Sat Yuga Press
Cover Design by:
Cartoonist: Smaradgi Magkou

Publisher: Sat Yuga Press. 132 Wilbur Hill Rd.
Unadilla, NY 13849 USA

*The information in this book is for educational purposes
only. It is not intended to treat, diagnose, prescribe, or
cure any health condition. For all health issues you are
advised to consult a qualified health care professional*

Dedication

Joy is our birthright.

This book is for all people who feel unsure and/or guilty about feeling joy in their lives, and feeling joy for no particular reason other than they choose to feel joyous.

How to Grow Your Joyful Paradise

What we put our attention on grows.
Choose what you love to do in the world
Choose what brings you inner peace & joy,
This is how you create your paradise. This
is how you live in your joy.
Joy, Joy, Joy!
— Swami Sadashiva Tirtha

Acknowledgements

This book was inspired by my students who want more joy in life, and to the late Marilou Trask-Curtain and the *Pleasant Valley Angels Writers Group* for their loving and helpful advice.

And to everyone who played a part in bringing this book to fruition.

This 2nd edition now includes a new set of cartoons drawn by Smaragdi Magkou. They add much joy and better convey the ideas in this book.

God grant me the serenity to accept the things I cannot change, the courage to change the things I can, and the wisdom to know the difference.
                              — Reinhold Niebuhr

I0157634

3

Twas the Night Before Joy...

Well, it is at least the moment before you embark on your journey to discover and/or grow your inner joy.

Research has found that when you repeat a new action or thought for 21 days, new brain pathways are created, making it a habit - something that you do automatically. So for the next 21 days by thinking joyful thoughts and doing things that bring you joy, you will quickly develop joyful neural pathways; it will be easier to think, act, and live with joy.

By following these joy exercises your brain muscle gets into shape. It's much easier to lift ideas than to life weights. And like physical exercise, the first few days you may feel your brain is sore. But by the fourth day, it is getting easier and the stiffness goes away.

I've arranged each day with a mantra or aphorism, something to think about throughout the day that will help you find

yourself, find some inner peace, and discover more joy in your life. You may even discover and fulfill your highest visions of how you can live in your own joyful paradise.

The goal of following ideas in this book is to exchange our thoughts that limit joy by connecting you more deeply to your soul. You should begin to feel the changes — instantly — in your health, emotions, and in your worldly activities.

Also, it will be very empowering for you to keep a journal of your ideas, feelings, and dreams starting from Day 1. Journaling helps us take our own council and allow us to take more control of our life.

May you discover ever more joy in your life!

Day 1
Dare to Feel Scared

It's ok to feel scared

There are two types of fear; fear of stepping out of the familiar or safe; and fear to try; fear to live.

It is healthy and natural to feel afraid of growing – trying something new

Everyone who works past healthy fear feels it create the adrenaline to achieve.

Those who give in to the fear to try die a little each time; do less with their lives, and their self-worth declines.

Unhealthy fear keeps us frozen

Feeling fear often results in us trying to look tough, but this cuts us off from our heart and inner knowing or wisdom

If you were deprived of true happiness or love as a child, you have the opportunity now to give it to yourself.

Have the courage to do things that make us feel healthy & joyful

Focus on your visions, not your fears

Exercises:

Read biographies and autobiographies of people you admire and wish to be like, and discover the same fears and vulnerabilities you have, in your heroes.

Make a list of the things that make you happy. Write down the next steps to feeling that happiness. You've just created long- & short-term goals.

Day 2
Healthy Food
Joyful Thoughts & Mood

Research has shown white sugar & junk food make us lose control of our thoughts

Eating junk foods is linked to drugs and other illegal actions

Bad foods cause bad moods

Feelings become agitated, worried, and fearful

Behavior become impatient and angry

When people eat whole grains and beans, fresh fruit, veggies, and dairy, their minds, emotions and behavior are more peaceful, clear, and joyful

Studies show people who eat whole foods do not become second-time offenders, and those who return to junk food return to law-breaking activities.

Give yourself the edge. Give yourself a foundation for a peaceful, joyful, successful life.

It's difficult to make positive changes mentally unless you make physical changes.

Exercise, eat right, get fresh air & sunlight. Spend time in nature as much as possible.

Exercises

Visit your local health food store or fresh produce section of your grocery store.

Recommended Reading
- *Food & Behavior* by Barbara Reed Stitt
- *Feeding the Brain* by C. Keith Conners
- *They are What You Feed Them* by Dr.

Alex Richardson
- *Ayurveda Encyclopedia* by Swami Sadashiva Tirtha
- *The Failsafe Cookbook* by Sue Dengate

Recommended Sites
Food and Behavior Research website (offers support, resources, bookstore, links to research, and support.
http://www.fabresearch.org

My site for beginner meditation & instant energy healing. http://OrangeCowboy.com

Experiment with eating healthy foods, even for a little, you will start feeling more balanced and healthy within 3-4 days

Day 3
Exercise - Energy Flies

Exercise creates endorphins in your brain that make you happy.

Do yoga, tai chi, karate, etc. They create mind/body coordination, bring peace of mind, and tone your muscles for inner strength.

Yoga and similar practices help heal pains, stiffness, and illness; and connect you to your spirit.

People find yoga helps them have more patience in daily life; big things seem to become little with a life practice of yoga or tai chi.

If you can't get out of bed, massage your body from head to toe. This exercises your body.

Walk, swim, or other exercise for a half-hour 4-6 days a week

Exercise

Exercise.

Seriously, walk outside, massage, stretch.

Nothing strenuous is required

See if your mood doesn't change after a few minutes

See if you feel more alive.

Day 4
Connect to
Nature & Pets
Joyful Life You'll Get

Mother nature heals our body & mind & touches our soul

Spending time in nature makes us feel connection to something greater than us

In nature we see we are a part of something bigger and not alone

Don't race; live at nature's pace

Spend a few days away from TV, radio, newspapers, cell phones, computers; and just experience how nature flows.

Cats, dogs, and other pets help soothe our emotions.

Pets seem to detect our mood and comfort us

Exercise:

- Smell the air - can you detect grass, or cows?
- Smell the earth - does it help you feel settled?
- Listen to the waterfall, stream, ocean - do you feel calm?
- Watch the daily movement of the sun, moon & stars
- Can you spot wild animals in nature?
- Notice the more alert we are in nature with so many sights and sounds

Day 5
Meditate:
Joy Won't Wait
You're Your Own
Best Soul Mate

Meditate on these ideas:

Ask,
'Who am I?'
Be true to yourself.
Be yourself - you are the most interesting person you know!

Pray to God (spirit, nature, etc.) to feel more connected and learn more about yourself and your purpose on the planet

Ask,
'What is my life purpose'
What brings me joy?
What centers me?
What calms me?

Where would I love to live (ocean, mountains, forest, desert, etc.)?
What would I love to do?

Smile & say hello to all you meet

Find something nice to say to people you meet

Ask,
'If I could live in paradise, where would it be and what would I do'?

...Now start working toward that vision...
You can do it!

Day 6
A Joyful Life
Makes Many Mistakes

If you're not making mistakes, you're not trying

Ok, maybe you were mistreated when you made mistakes in your life - yelled at, ignored, laughed at, or worse. But that is their issue. Do not let others define you.
You are soul, eternal spirit, child of God. You were born with original grace. But only you can discover that.

Life is for learning; it is an adventure – an experiment. Choose to see life in this way and you create life on your terms.

Hang with positive friends who support your

vision and you support theirs.

When we take ourselves too seriously and the joy in our life drains away.

It is not for us to shoulder the weight of the world, but to feel playful and share a loving world with others - a give and take - a sharing of one another's strengths.

Laugh at the small mistakes or else they build up to a serious mistake that winds up hurting yourself and/or others, and then it is no longer a laughing matter.

Once you learn from a mistake, it transforms from a mistake into a life lesson. There is no regret.

Exercises
In your journal write down mistakes you

made in your life. Make two columns, one for minor mistakes that were barely noticeable, and one column for serious mistakes that affected the lives of others.

a) Looking back on them, write down what you learned from them?

b) At the times of the minor mistakes, you may have felt your world miserable. Can you find something funny about that situation that you can laugh at now?

Or do you feel that what you once thought was the end of the world, now seems like no big deal?

Can you see how those mistakes were blessings in disguise for you?

c) Reviewing the life-altering mistakes, can you find an earlier set of mistakes of judgment that you ignored that changed your behavior to lose joy and playfulness?

Day 7
Find the Joy
Without Hesitation
to Change the Sad in All
Situations

Try your best to change an unwanted situation without unduly stressing yourself out. If it doesn't change accept it and seek to understand how you can use the situation to improve something in your life.

Change your view of 'bad' events; see them as a 'challenges' or 'opportunities'.

If you have tried your best to change an undesirable situation, and it doesn't change, ask, 'What can I learn from this situation?'

'Bad' situations are undesirable, but they can teach us patience, understanding, empathy, and compassion.

Success comes from within, using your innate abilities or God gifts.

It is difficult to make excuses for our lives when we see people with similar challenges in their life succeed to the highest levels of life:

<u>ADHD</u>: Tommy Hilfiger, Terry Bradshaw, Michael Phelps

<u>Dyslexia</u>: Cher, Danny Glover, Henry Winkler, Magic Johnson, Whoopi Goldberg, Walt Disney

<u>Stuttering</u>: Bruce Willis, Julia Roberts, Mel Tillis, Samuel L Jackson, Winston Churchill

<u>People in Wheelchairs</u>: Stephen Hawking, Teddy Pendergrass, President F.D. Roosevelt, Itzhak Perlman

<u>Obsessive Compulsive Disorders</u>: Donald Trump, Cameron Diaz, Leonardo Dicaprio, Michael Jackson

<u>Asthma</u>: Elizabeth Taylor, Alice Cooper, Bob Hope, Judy Collins

<u>Mood Disorders</u>: Harrison Ford, Carrie Fisher, Billy Joel, Boris Yeltsin, Jim Carrey, Brooke Shields

<u>Alcohol and Drug Addiction</u>: Eric Clapton, Jason Pollock, Betty Ford, Craig Ferguson, Kris Kristofferson

Exercise
Read biographies of people who have had tremendous obstacles in life similar to yours (or succeeding in a career you would love to work in) and overcame them, creating something to help the world or winning a competition

Day 8
Don't Take Yourself
Too Seriously

Laugh at Yourself

Act a Little Silly or Crazy

When we're playful life is softer, easier

Find a balance between listening to your heart and mind.

Beware of believing you are a savior. It's the beginning of a hard fall.

When people tell you that you are crazy, thank them; it is a sign you are expressing your unique individuality

People live life too seriously; media mostly reports serious, fearful, dire news. Take a break and add some fresh air each day; add some silliness

Exercises

Simple things to change your energy:

Make a funny face

Speak in a funny voice

Skip down the road

Sing out loud to the sky or mountains or water that you love them
 Shout out to God in gratitude for a glorious day, or just to be alive

Express your joy at least a little bit each day

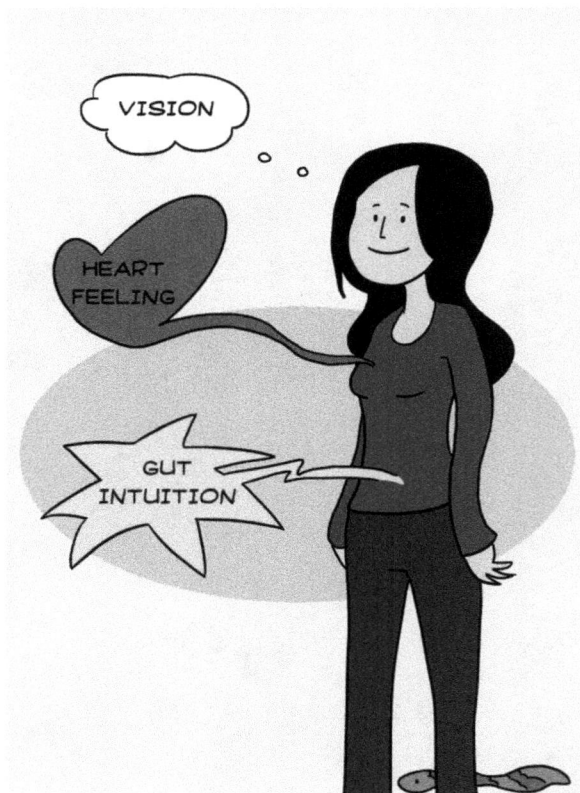

38

Day 9
Advice is Nice
Listen to Intuition

It is always helpful to get advice from people who have been down the road you're on — mentor or club, (eg, writers' group).

After listening to qualified people's advice, then check with your own intuition; how do you feel about the options? Let your intuition have the final word.

Ask your angels, guides, or God (whatever you believe in) for guidance. You should 'feel' or 'know' or 'hear' when an answer is best for you.

The wisest teacher is your intuition

If you don't understand what someone is

saying, ask them to clarify

People have different definitions for the same word. Make sure you understand each other's definitions

The first sign of wisdom is admitting you don't know

Exercises
When asking for advice, start with the words, 'How can I..." so your mind starts open to the fact that it can be done

If you ask 'Can I...' you start from a place of doubt?

examples:
'How can I find more peace in life'

'How can I find a more enjoyable job?'

"How can I find more love in my relationship?"

"How can I get accomplish my goals & visions?"

Day 10
Whatever You Do
Comes Back to You

Life is like a ball; whatever you do & say, kind or hurtful, it bounces back

This is a universal law; If you hurt or love someone physically, verbally, or emotionally, that hurt or love will return to your life

Like a pond - throw a rock in one area and waves reach the entire pond, and then return

Wish everyone well, an enemy whose heart opens ceases to cause you trouble

The Bible says, 'as you sow, so shall you reap'

Modern day science says 'every action has an equal opposite reaction'

Keep your word or all get hurt: People will make plans based on what you say you will do. If you suddenly back out only because you want to, lives get disrupted and people can't trust you.

Doing what you say is solid gold integrity

Exercises

Look around for people and places that make you happy and open hearted and avoid the people and places that cause you negativity.

Watch your thoughts—are they positive or negative, hopeful or without faith, sincere or cynical? Consciously work to think, say and do harmonious things - even if they are not how you feel. Within three days, you will start to feel harmonious as you say them.

Train your mind (see diagram below) to think or believe your words and habits to be as kind and open hearted as best you can, and you will find yourself living in a happy, kind, open hearted world

Day 11
Attitude of Gratitude

Be grateful for the good things in life

When you're grateful more good things happen for you

Even when life is tough, when you look for things to be grateful for in life, you begin to feel better

An attitude of gratitude makes life more meaningful

If we are not grateful, we find nothing to be happy about, and so we are stuck with that unhappy life

Gratitude is a sign of wealth; Cultivate the virtue of gratitude

There is something in everyone's life to be grateful for

Training your thoughts to be grateful is mental exercise; the first few days are painful; thereafter it gets easier.

Exercises

When we go to sleep at night, think of things during the day you are grateful for (eg, health, friends, sunshine, being alive...).

Make a mental note or better still, write it in your journal.

Examples of how to see the best in every situation:
If life gets tough, say it could be worse
Think of 5 people who have it tougher than you do
Think of 1 country where people have it tougher than you

Day 12
Learn Earns Joy

Be forever a student of life

Life runs more smoothly when we have more questions than answers

When we are in 'learning mode' we are sincere and humble. When we think we know everything, that is the crucial fork in the path that leads us to ruin

Some days everything goes our way. Other days are challenges. Life is cyclical; be careful to not think one good day means you've 'made it'

When you can accept learning on the smooth days and the challenging days life goes more

smoothly
 Thinking you know takes you out of your
heart

Feeling is a state of wonder and awe; unsure
yet exciting

It is easier to drop to the heart than to rise to
the brain

Exercise

Choose a subject that you would love to learn and start studying it; either for free online (eg, how to play piano on YouTube), adult education or library courses, college courses, one-on-one training with a teacher

Choose things that you love to do, for the sheer fun of it; don't worry that you're not good at it or don't think you can make a living

Examples include writing, painting or drawing, playing a music instrument, knitting/yarn, dancing

Day 13
Gleaning
Your Life's Meaning

When life is meaningful, we feel a flow of happiness, energy, and confidence

Doing what we love makes us feel purposeful

Everything is easier in purpose - rolling downhill

People are attracted to you when you do what you love; relationships are sweeter

People will pay you for doing what you love

It doesn't get any better than that!

Exercise

Open your journal to a new page. Write the topic headline: "Things I Love to Do"

And list them; one thing, 3 things; 8 things... Let your heart flow.

Write things you love, even if you're not good at them

List loves even if you think you can't make a living with them

If you have an overly rational or critical or logical mind, tell it to wait in the next room for a half-hour and then you'll be back.

Write from your heart!

Write from your gut feelings!

When done, prioritize them.
What do you most love?

Once in priority, start doing the first one - a

little each day - 10 minutes, half-hour. Just for fun. Keep doing this until priority number 2 calls for attention and do that for some time.

See Day 12 for how to share what you love

Day 14
Share What You Love
Blest from Above

Do what you love and your cup fills and runneth over with peace and joy, confidence and playfulness.

Others soak in your overflowing joy and your joy is amplified; you feel greater divine blessings

Choose to be around people who will not crush your dreams and heart

Choose people who, like you, have dreams, are doing what they love

These people can be mentors or friends or family - usually mentors are best to seek out.

Share your ideas with professionals in the field you love and show them your work (eg, art, music, carpentry, cooking, etc.).

Volunteer and share your gifts to help an event, organization or a person or group that will appreciate what you love.

Join or create a support group of like-minded people. The role of the group is to offer loving support and give constructive advice—no negative thoughts during the meeting.

Share your work with children if it is appropriate (ie, engine repair may not interest a child). Children often offer the best feedback and advice

The more you share what you love, the more stoked you get, and the more you see how your gifts make others happy too.

The gift of sharing your gifts is discovering greater faith in yourself and your gifts.

Exercise

Where to Share
Start with your local newspapers and chamber of commerce. Ask for a list of non-profit organizations

Call the ones that have an interest in what you love to do. Offer them a free demonstration, talk, help etc. (eg, help building houses for Habitat for Humanity; drawing pictures at an orphanage).
Sing & Play at open-mic nights

Post your artistic endeavors online at YouTube and other video sites

Create a web page and offer free advice and/or creative projects internationally

When you feel more confident, and you make a name for yourself as a helpful community member, the jobs offers will start coming in

Day 15
Exceptions Cause Deception

This time won't be different!

If you drink or speed, or take drugs, you will always undermine your life.

Every time you hammer your head it will hurt!
Every time you enter an unhealthy pattern you create downward cycle

This is because all things in life are a part of the cyclical, spiraling laws of nature - life returns to where it began - though on a new higher level (higher because of all the experiences we've had since the last start).

The same laws of nature apply to everyone. When you think you are different - that is a red flag telling you your ego has gone off its track.

We are all individuals, and we each have our

limitations. Honor your limits and grow your gifts. Limits keep us humble; gratitude for our gifts keeps us humble.

Better to follow your own path with its flaws than try to live another's path though it may seem perfect

Everyone needs to follow a basic set of rules - best they are universal laws and not manmade.

We don't have to be perfect. Only our soul is perfect, not our ideas, emotions, and behaviors

Exercise

<u>Treasure Map:</u>
<u>Listening with ears & intuition</u>
Here is a game to help you choose successful thought and actions and prevent undermining thoughts from tripping you up.

Using the illustration at the end of this exercise, open your journal or new game book and make a list of things you love to do that relate to the ideas in the drawing.

As long as you spend some time in each of these areas, daily, weekly, or even monthly, you will help yourself remain balanced because you will grow good feelings and creativity in all areas of your life.

If you neglect any area for too long, your heart will become sad, and if you continue to ignore this, eventually your heart will become angry and eventually do something for you to notice...ultimately tripping you up

Day 16
Understanding
Won't Help Planning

Schooling gives intelligence —Experience gives wisdom

Mind is theory, heart is experience. We must live from our hearts as well as our minds.

The final decisions are always best made with our intuition (feelings or gut reaction)

When we 'know', we are fooling ourselves - When we 'feel' something may be a certain way, we may be right

It is wisest to confirm 3 sources before considering what is the best thing to do: what a textual or scriptural authority says, what your mentor or advisor says, and what you experience. When all three corroborate, you can feel more confident it is a right choice

Its best to live in the state of not being sure

and feeling your way through life; following your visions

We can say, I act based on my inner visions and dreams. It is not a right or wrong situation

What we feel we are to do is different from other people's visions what they are called to do

Accept everyone and their paths, and still accept yourself and stick to your path

Be a living example of wisdom, not merely an orator of wise words.

Don't be a 'do and I say and not as I do' person; life becomes prideful and empty hearted.

Exercise
Examine your core beliefs.
What do you <u>'feel'</u> about each area of life:

1. What I feel about taking care of my health

_____

_____

_____

_____

2. What I feel about earning a living doing what I love to do

_____

_____

_____

_____

3. What I feel about helping the earth

_____

_____

_____

_____

4. What I feel about helping children

_____

_____

_____

_____

5. What I feel about nature

_____

_____

_____

_____

6. What I feel about people

_____

_____

_____

_____

LONG TERM GOALS

2010	2020	2030
2040	2050	2060
2070	2080	2090

Day 17
Long-Term Choice
You Rejoice

Choose things that last

Choose things that take root

Choose things that grow for your benefit

Choose things that help others while helping yourself

Choose healthy eating for long-term physical health

Choose healthy eating for long-term mental peace & joy

Choose careers where you will grow

Choose pleasures that open your mind and emotions,

Choose humans and feelings over machines and mechanical structures

Choose work you love rather than just for the money; when you have a miserable boss, no amount of money is worth the hassle.

Choose what you love to do to keep you in love with yourself, others and life 24/7

Choose thoughts that are harmonious and avoid thoughts of low self-esteem, doubt, and fear; anger, impatience, and laziness

Choose conversations that are pleasant; avoid gossip, backbiting, and complaining

Note there is a difference between short-term results (ie, instant gratification that prevents you from growing your life) and short-term goals (steps that lead you to reach long-term goals)

Exercise

In your journal make a list of choices that lead to short term and long term or <u>lasting</u> results.

For example:

Short Term: taking drugs, speeding, stealing, yelling, controlling, complaining, arguing, fighting, ignoring (responsibilities), eating junk foods, laziness, doing what you don't love, thinking you are all-knowing/all-powerful; going it alone, living artificially (indoors, air conditioning, no fresh air or exercise), not socializing at all

Long Term: gratitude, speaking kindly, loving others, accepting others, eating fresh foods, exercising, doing what you love, giving thanks to someone/thing greater than yourself (God, spirit, nature), volunteering, spending time in nature, seeking out mentors & trusted friend's advice, socialize — even if it is just with close family and friends.

Day 18
You Can Be Joyful
or You Can Be Right

Speaking self-righteously does not make you right

Judging other's beliefs blows up your ego and sets you up to crash

If you get agitated by someone doing something you think isn't supposed to be done, check your heart; you don't want to do it either

Do what brings joy and not what you are told you 'should' do *(this applies in context of law-abiding, long-term growth choices)*

Happy comes from heart; right comes from

self-imposed (false) rules

Exercise

Journal:
What are the topics and people you find you get most angry about?

For each topic and person, list what you feel is the reason you get angry.

Eg,
- Joe speeds in his car
- Frank can drink but I can't
- Dad thinks he knows everything
- Mom doesn't let me do anything
- No one listens to my ideas

For each issue, ask yourself if it is worth you getting upset, or would you rather be feeling joyful.

Ask: How can I move on to do something I love and let go of what other people think and feel? How can l accept we have different views and habits and live my life?

Day 19
What You See,
Becomes Your Reality

If you think you can you can—If you think you can't you can't

What you tell yourself is reality is what you look for to prove your belief.

Think of the greatest paradise you can imagine for yourself and it will slowly come to pass

When you get stuck, ask 'how can I get free?'

Dream the biggest dream for yourself—God brings you something even bigger

Look to the vision in your mind's eye what your paradise looks like

Exercise

Try telling yourself new beliefs that you would like to believe even if you feel they are fantasy

Eg,

- Life is as good as I want it to be
- I experience miracles in life
- I see joy and can live joy
- I love myself
- I can achieve my visions
- I am worthy
- I accept myself just as I am
- I don't need to fight or argue just to prove what I believe - its just my beliefs, not another's.
- Be kind for its own sake; help others is its own reward

After a few days, you likely will start seeing these beliefs appear in your life

Soon you will believe these views because they become a daily reality

Day 20
Dreams Teach Us Things

Do you remember your dreams?

Do your dreams sometimes come true in life; do the dreams warn you or prepare you in some way for your next day?

Do some dreams seem as real as life (or more real?)

Consider your dreams as messages or visions that can guide you to find a life more peaceful and joyful

Listen to your daydreams in the same way, they are pointing you to a magical life.

Dreams are mystical communication with your highest self!

Exercises

Keep a dream journal by your bed. If you wake up after the dream, write it down. If you wake up in the morning and remember a dream, write it down

Meditate on what the dream may mean; use your feelings and intuition to discover the meaning (ie, was it a dream saying be concerned, or simply get ready, you're in for a change).

If you need, ask for help interpreting the dreams from angels, mentors, spirit, nature, God (etc.)

Day 21
Be the Change
You Wish to See
You'll Live a Joyous Reality

A good measure of whether you are headed for success or headed for a crash is to see who/what you are focused on.

If you are trying to change others, you're headed for trouble.

If you're trying to change yourself in healthy ways, and if you are accepting yourself for who you are, this is healthy

Self-love and acceptance, living as much of your peace and paradise, doing what you love to do, and living your joy is a life practice; it never ends

There is no 'done' when growing your joy and paradise, just as there is no done when you love someone.

It just keeps getting deeper, special and joyful

Exercise
<u>Journal</u>: Make a list of all the things you like about yourself in green ink and don't like about yourself in blue ink

- Check to ensure you are not being critical of yourself needlessly on any issue

- List your strengths in green and weaknesses in blue

- Scan yourself to make sure you are not judging yourself.

- Tell yourself you are grateful for all the things you like about yourself, and all your God-gifts or innate abilities.

- Tell yourself you love yourself as you are; with all the things that make up your personality.

- Review your strengths and your vision for your peace and paradise, and ask, 'How can I use my gifts to live more of my paradise.

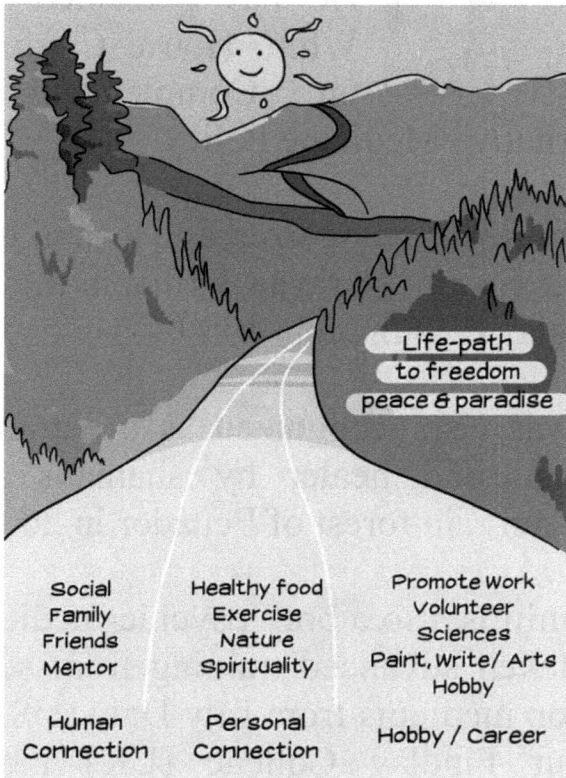

Life-path
to freedom
peace & paradise

Social	Healthy food	Promote Work
Family	Exercise	Volunteer
Friends	Nature	Sciences
Mentor	Spirituality	Paint, Write/ Arts
		Hobby
Human	Personal	
Connection	Connection	Hobby / Career

About the Author

Swami Sadashiva Tirtha is the author of the Amazon #1 bestseller in its category, the *Ayurveda Encyclopedia.*

He has presented to the White House Commission on Complementary & Alternative Medicine Policy.

Swamiji was recognized as a swami by his guruji, Swami Narayan Tirtha, in the Himalayas of India in 1990.

He was also recognized as a natural-born shaman and healer by shamans in the Amazon rain forest of Ecuador in 2008.

Swamiji is also a born psychic-medium and has taken advanced training from some of the top mediums from Lily Daly (USA) and Arthur Findlay College (UK) including James Van Praagh, Tony Stockwell, Lisa Williams, Janet Nohavec, and Sharon

Klingler.

Cowboy Swami Shaman, or the Orange Cowboy, as he is known, began teaching meditation and yoga in 1976.

Swamiji earned the first Doctor of Science in Ayurveda research in the USA.

His other books include the *Bhagavad Gita for Modern Times,* and his latest book, *The Stress-Free College Student* that Bryant University lists on their Pinterest page next to their '50 Books that Changed the World'.

Beginner Meditation Course

Swamiji has distilled his 4 decades of teaching meditation into a simple beginner meditation method that gives advance results. Instant Energy & Healing through the Heart Method guides even newbies to have instant and profound relief, energy, and joy from their meditation.

Experience results at home or while on the go; from 1 minute to 1 hour. Everyone can meditate. [Online/At your event]

Group Mediumship
Swamiji offers live events to reconnect you with loved ones who have departed, and your angels, guides, and masters. He offers solid specific stories spirit shares with him that only you could know. This evidence helps you feel this is really coming from your loved ones.

Mediumship messages heals grief, guilt, and help give you your life back to you. It also helps prove that there is live after life. This is a very healing and sacred experience.

[Online web events & at your event]

Shamanic Energy Healing
Swamiji incorporates his gifts of energy healing in his meditation course and mediumship sessions. Experience instant relief from emotion-physical-relationship-career stressors.

Connect with Swamiji and experience your

life transform in an instant. Details at
http://OrangeCowboy.com

Other Books by Swamiji

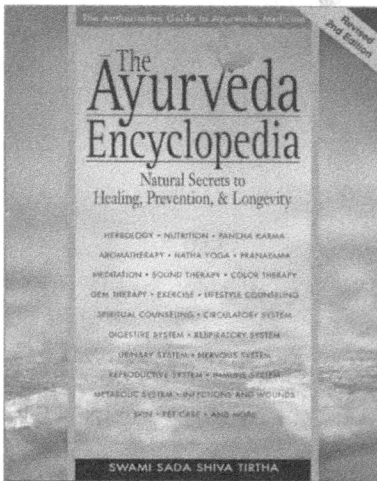

Amazon #1 bestseller; 30,000 copies in print. The *bible* of Ayurveda. Covers the history, theory, and thousands of health issues. Includes foods, herbs, yoga, color therapy, aromatherapy, for pets and much more.

EDITOR'S CHOICE! *"... a comprehensive, detailed primer for serious students of Ayurveda, (yet) its design and layout is also "lay-person-friendly:" Indeed it is one of the better...texts...; clarifies)...Ayurveda for the Western readers ...provides a deeper insight into the spiritual foundations of Ayurveda; a complete analysis of how diseases are caused and...progress...Best of all (the) approach is refreshingly honest.*" The Bodhi Tree Review

"*You could buy a half-dozen plus books on Ayurveda to start your reference library, or you could buy...(this) Encyclopedia. It's detailed enough for the professional, but accessible to the lay person...It is useful and entertaining for any student of Ayurveda or as a home self-healing resource...(a) magnum opus.*" Hinduism Today

"*...you'll be delighted to discover this comprehensive guide...*" Herb Research News (Herb Research Foundation)

"*...an important reference volume for all students of Ayurveda and Yoga, almost a complete course in Ayurveda in itself. Swami Sadashiva Tirtha has done a monumental work in putting together so much material in such a concise and clear manner for the modern reader.*" — Dr. David Frawley (Vamadeva Shastri); Director: American Institute of Vedic Studies

"For me, this is the next best book after Harrison's Internal Medicine Text. I think every doctor should read this book for better insights into the entire psycho-physiologic makeup of his or her patients" — Patrick J. Conte MD; Radiologist - New Jersey

"...gives a (spiritual) perspective that is lacking in the current alternative literature." — Robert Pincus, MD

"...a 'must have' reference for any health professional involved in integrative medicine." — Ellen Kamhi PhD RN HNC ("The Natural Nurse")/Author

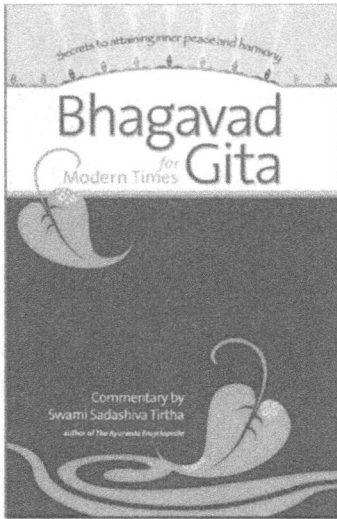

"Exceptional ...easy to follow workbook... relates to the modern society... especially suitable as a text for Gita workshop." — Bhupendra Hajratwala, Ph.D. President, North American Hindu Association

"It made me understand my relationship with God...first Gita my child has read." — Kul B. Anand, MD FRCP London. Exec. Member, India Assn. of Long Island, NY

"Builds friendly bridges across millennia and cultures to the Gita's counsel...with a giving spirit Krishna would recognize." — Bill Drayton, Chair/CEO, Ashoka

"The first Gita I understood, and immediately applied it to my life and

practice…'must read' book for my clients."
— Michael I. Gurevich, MD, Psychiatrist

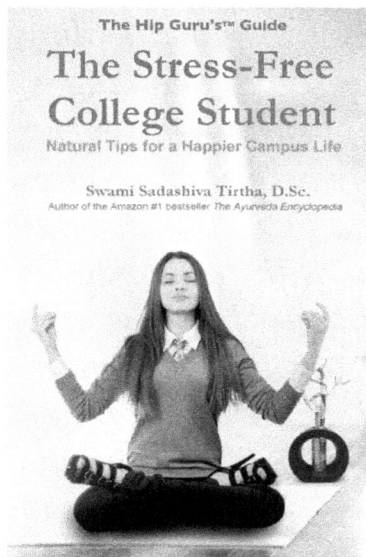

"If you follow Swami's wisdom and use his book as a resource, you can learn to control your life…He's a man of broad knowledge and deep wisdom — a generous and inspiring teacher. You will certainly learn much from him about your life in general and your life as a college student in particular. He shows you how to put your college life in order and how to find balance and harmony in your whole life."
— Dr. Bob. Neuman, Ph.D. Former Academic Dean, Marquette University

"East meets West in this wonderful guide, and college students will be the big winners.

College can be one big stress event for young people: living away from home, choosing majors, worrying about grades, meeting deadlines, taking tests, and dealing with an endless range of social challenges. Like the soothing sound of surf on a summer night, Swami Sadashiva Tirtha equips students with techniques, tips, and insights that will help them deal with the anxieties that can come with college life. Swamiji provides practical and inspiring solutions from yoga to Feng Shui. Not every solution will suit each student's personality and preferences, but everyone will find lots of valuable information that will help them cope and conquer the stresses of college life." Alfred Poor, PhD Author, 7 Success Secrets That Every College Student Needs to Know!

"Stress Free College Student Guide is a "must read" for all college students. Swamiji creates a comprehensive, detailed book for college students. The book itself is a stress-free inviting read to help students

step by step to find a way to step beyond the stressful, demanding mold that most students feel trapped in. It is a very user-friendly read for college students that can be read in one sitting and equip them with many relaxation techniques." — Pamela DeNeuve Author, The Handbook for Healing Heartbreak: Finding Peace Within, After Loss of Love

Swamiji's Services

Explore Swamiji's unique **Instant Energy & Healing through the Heart Method:**

1. Beginner Mediation Course (with advance Results)
   Everyone Can Meditate!
2. Group Mediumship Events
3. Shamanic Instant Energy Trance Healing

All services are available online and at events in your location

Websites

TheHipGurusGuide.com

OrangeCowboy.com

Boost your love, happiness, harmony, and prosperity with astrology sessions

I found by following your astrology blueprint your energy flows, life has more meaning, and fills with joy - Swamiji

Home   Love Locations   Compatibility   Life Readings   Birthday   Forecast   Business   Business Bulls-Eye   Sports

Online Astrology Readings ▾   Testimonials   Blog   Contact Us

My Astrology Session
Your blueprint for life

MyAstrologySession.com

Connect with me on Social Media

— *Like/Follow/Subscribe*

Facebook.com/MonkMedium

Twitter.com/MonkMedium

bit.ly/OrangeCowboyYT

linkedin.com/in/SwamiSadashivaTirtha

Instagram.com/MonkMedium

bit.ly/OrangeCowboyGPlus

Pinterest.com/MonkMedium/

monkmedium.tumblr.com